# The Barking Lot
## Underwater Coloring Book

# The Barking Lot
# Underwater Coloring Book

KF Wheatie & KM Wheatie

Strawberryhead &
Gingerbread Press

www.strawberryheadandgingerbread.com

The Barking Lot Underwater Coloring Book

Published by Strawberryhead and Gingerbread Press
https://www.strawberryheadandgingerbread.com

Copyright © 2024 by KF Wheatie & KM Wheatie

All rights reserved. Neither this book, nor any parts within it may be sold or reproduced in any form or by any electronic or mechanical means, including information storage and retrieval systems, without permission in writing from the author. The only exception is by a reviewer, who may quote short excerpts in a review.

ISBN: 979-8-9906129-1-4 (paperback)

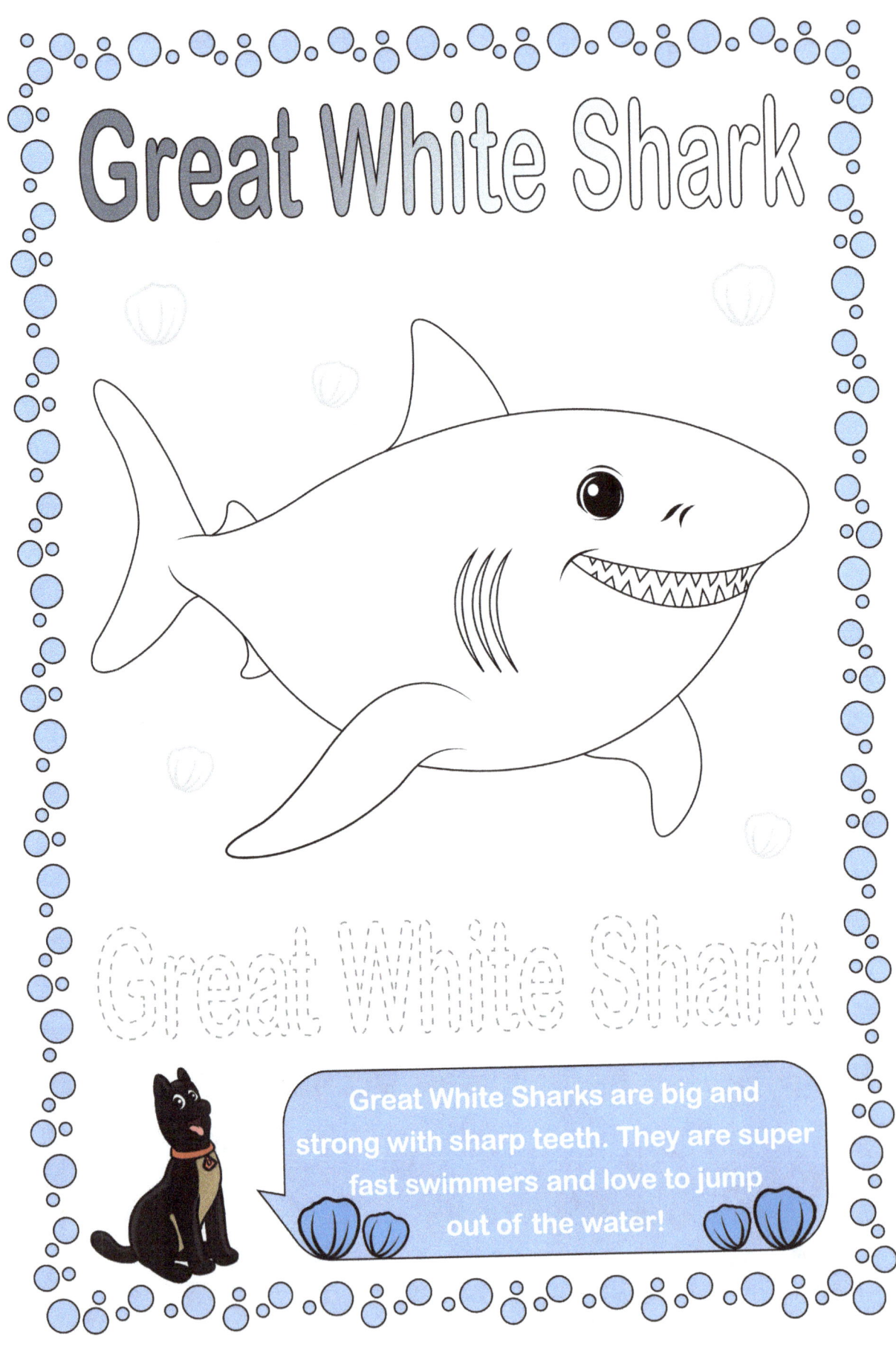

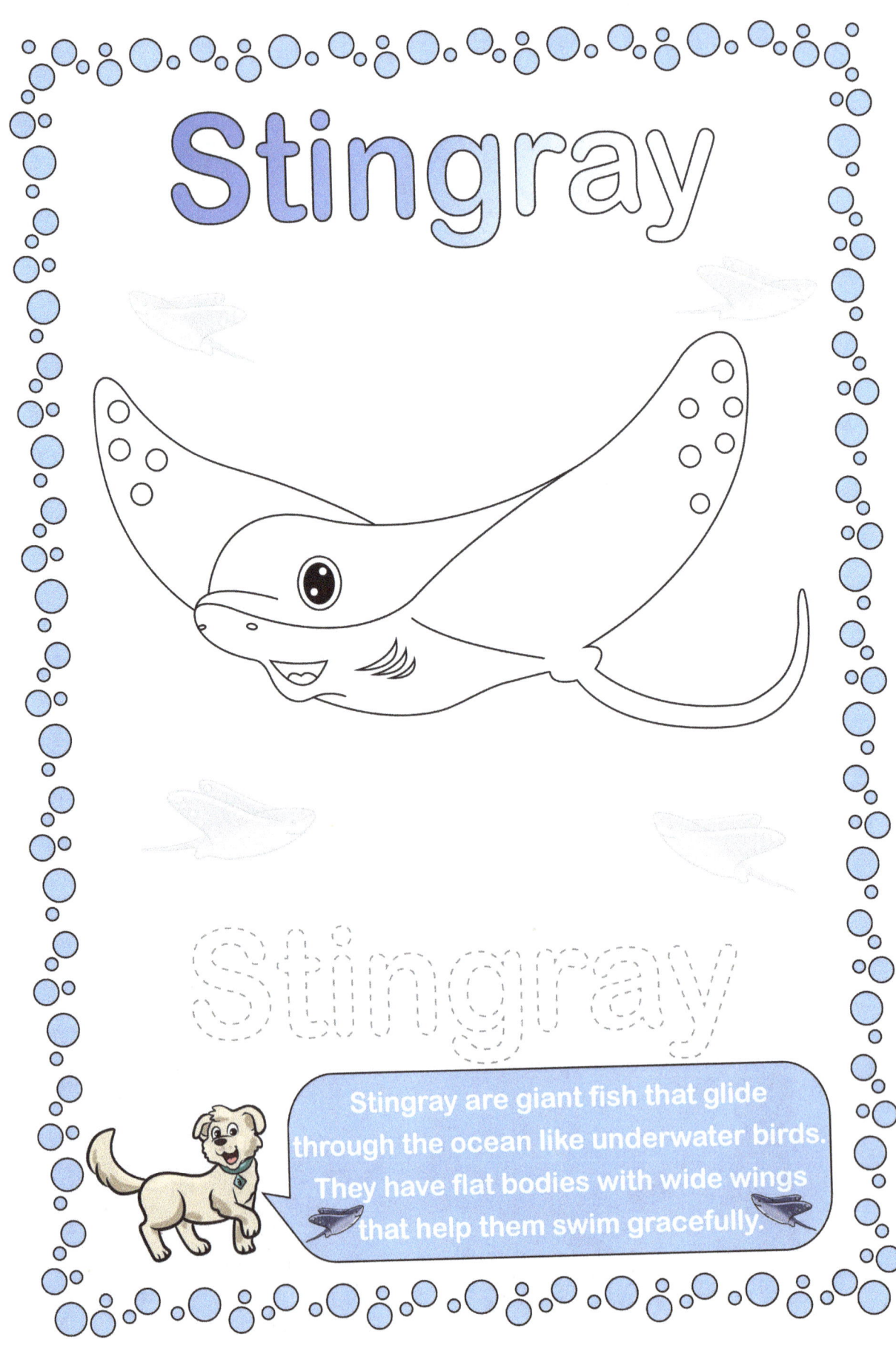

# Lobsters

Lobsters have big claws and hard shells. They crawl along the ocean floor using their legs. Their claws are strong & help them catch their meals.

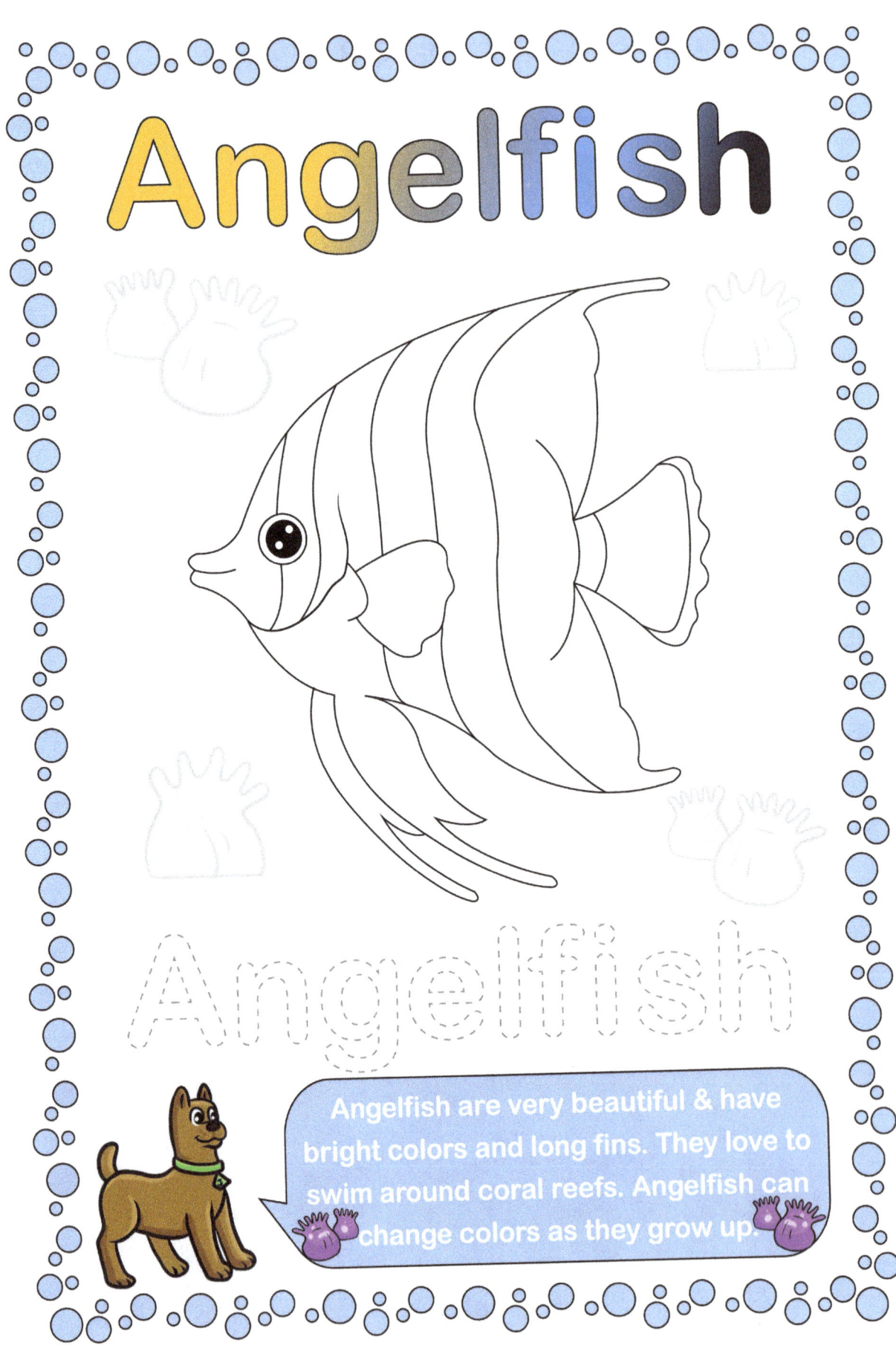

# Angelfish

Angelfish are very beautiful & have bright colors and long fins. They love to swim around coral reefs. Angelfish can change colors as they grow up.

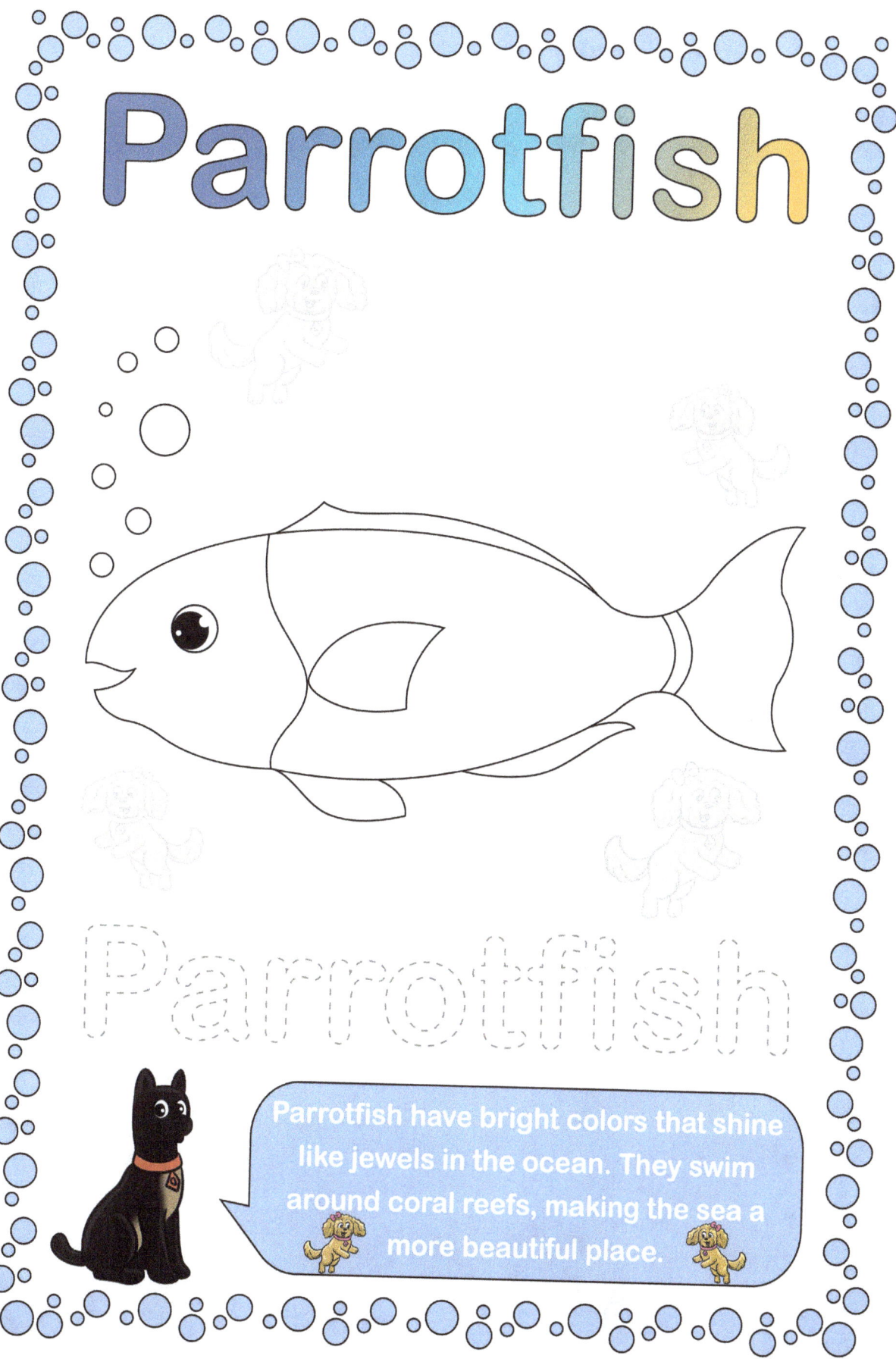

# Pufferfish

Pufferfish

Pufferfish are like little balloons that can inflate in the ocean. Some pufferfish are even poisonous, which helps keep them safe from predators.

# Lionfish

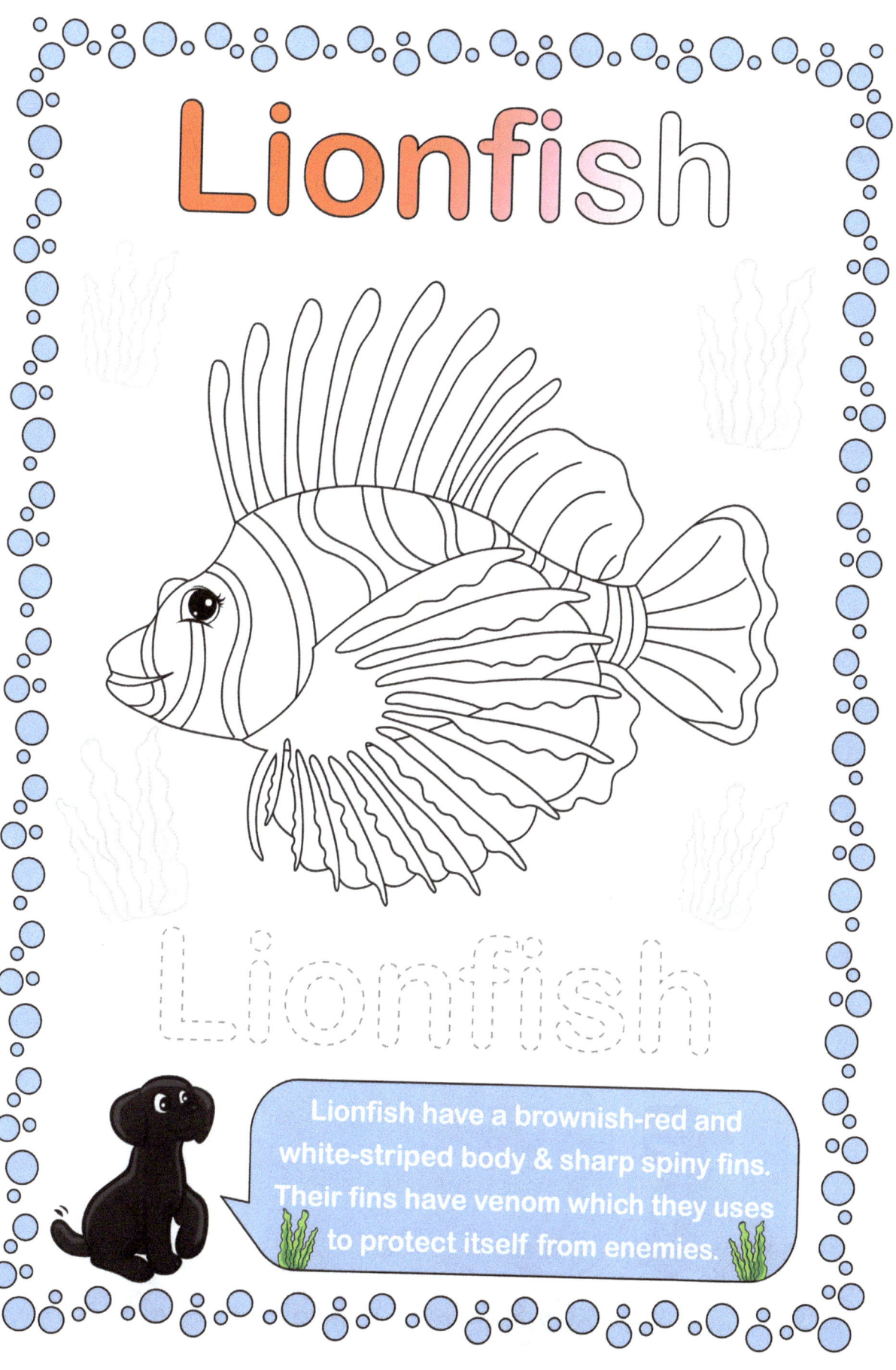

Lionfish

Lionfish have a brownish-red and white-striped body & sharp spiny fins. Their fins have venom which they uses to protect itself from enemies.

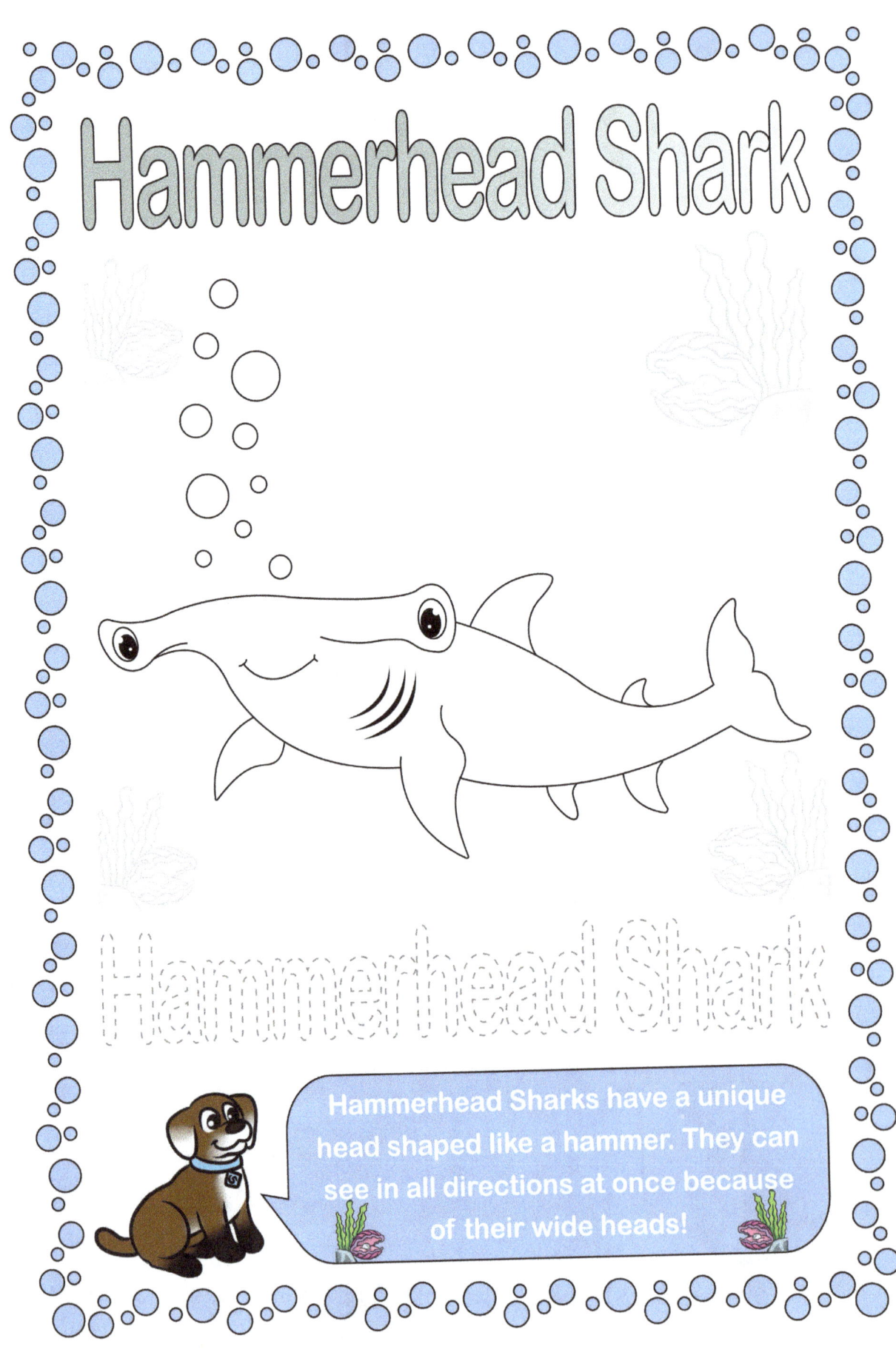

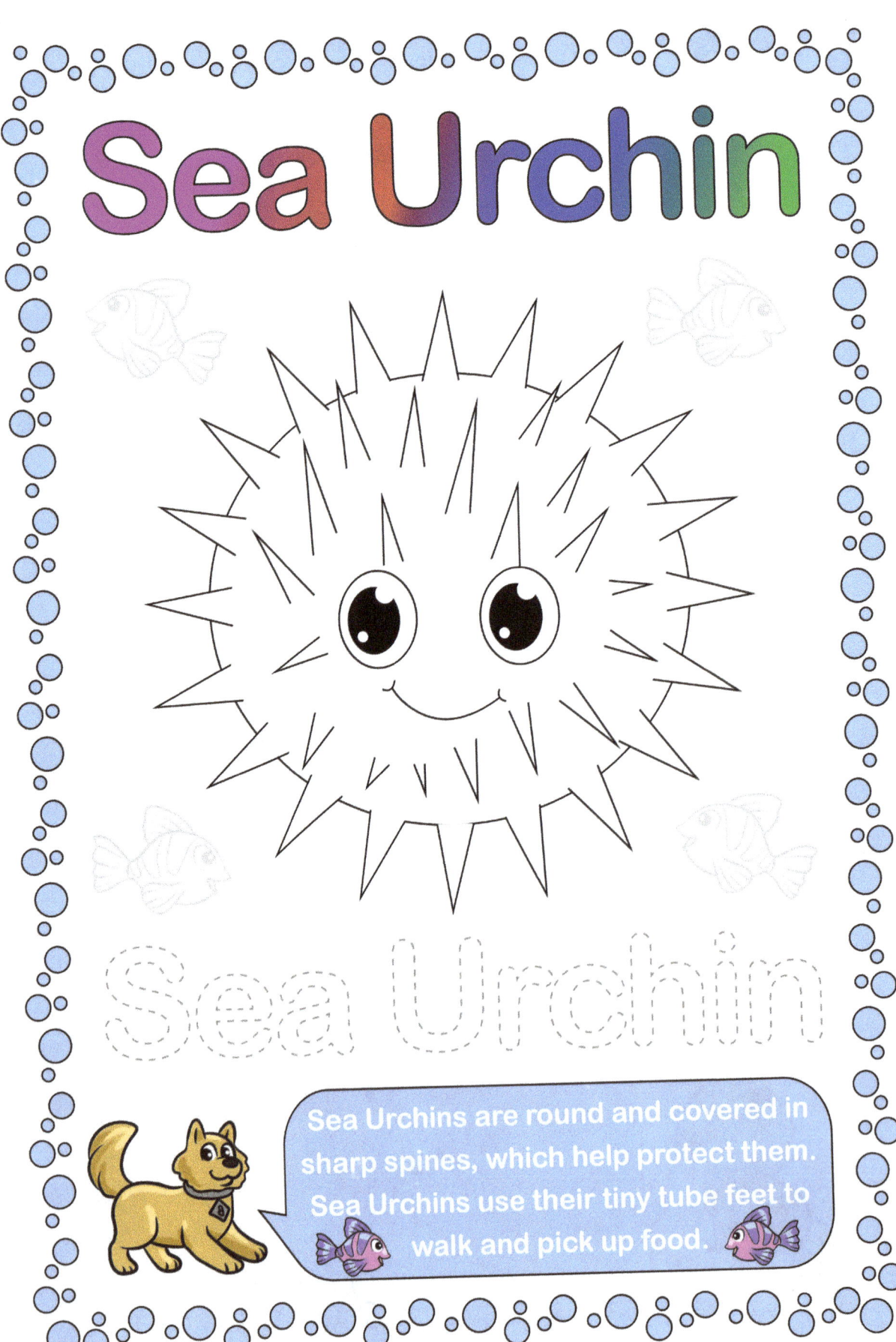

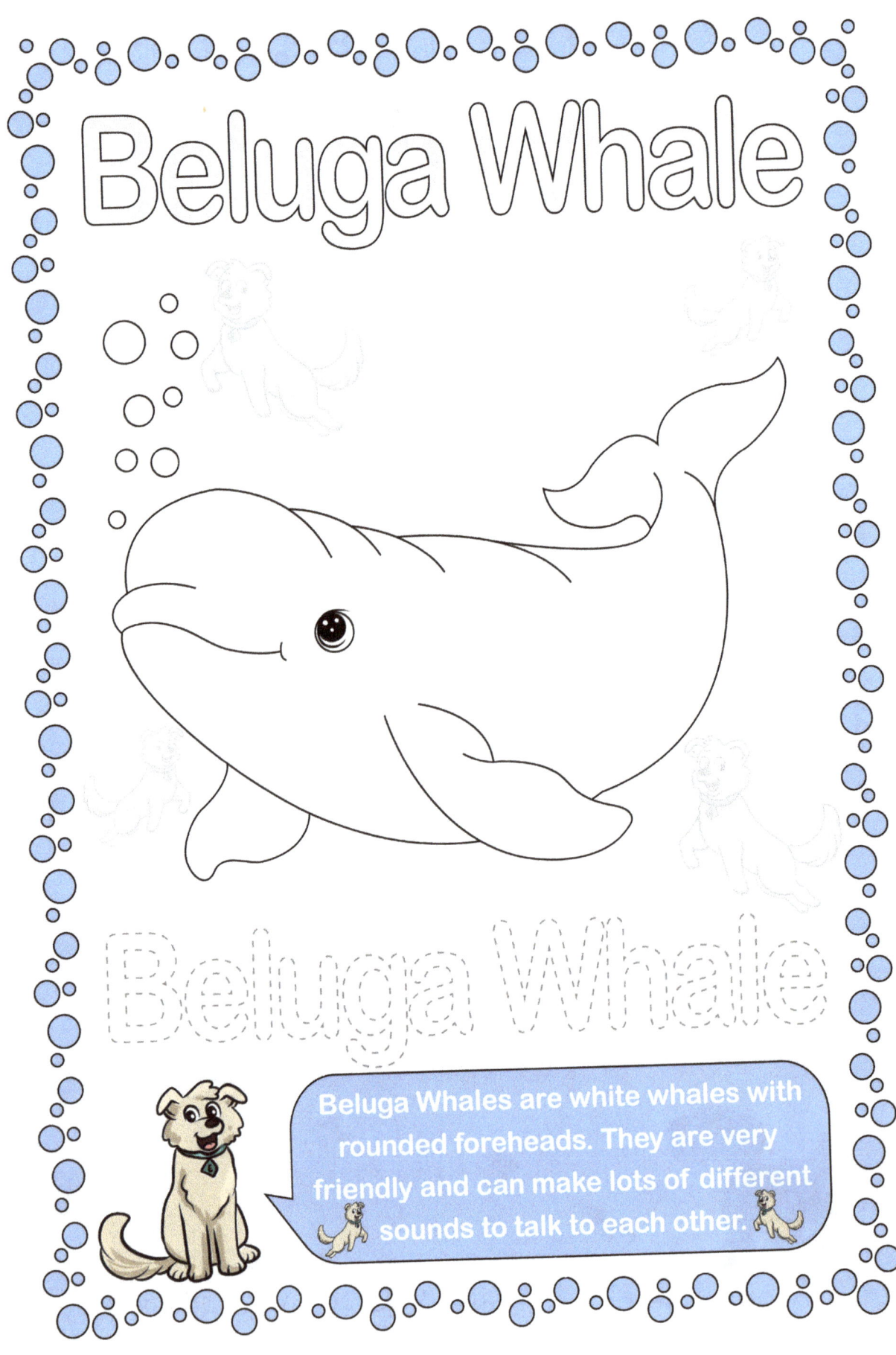

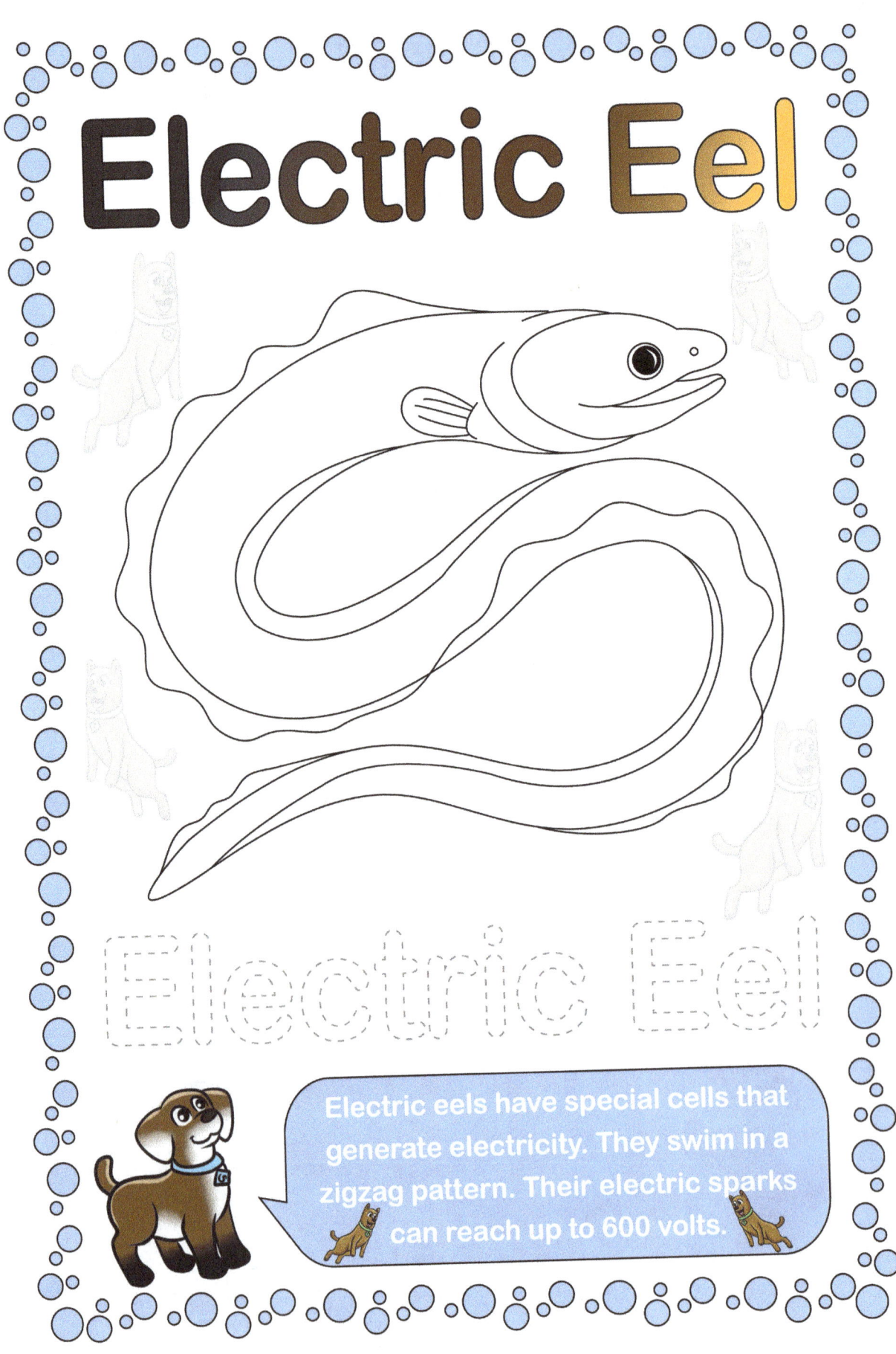

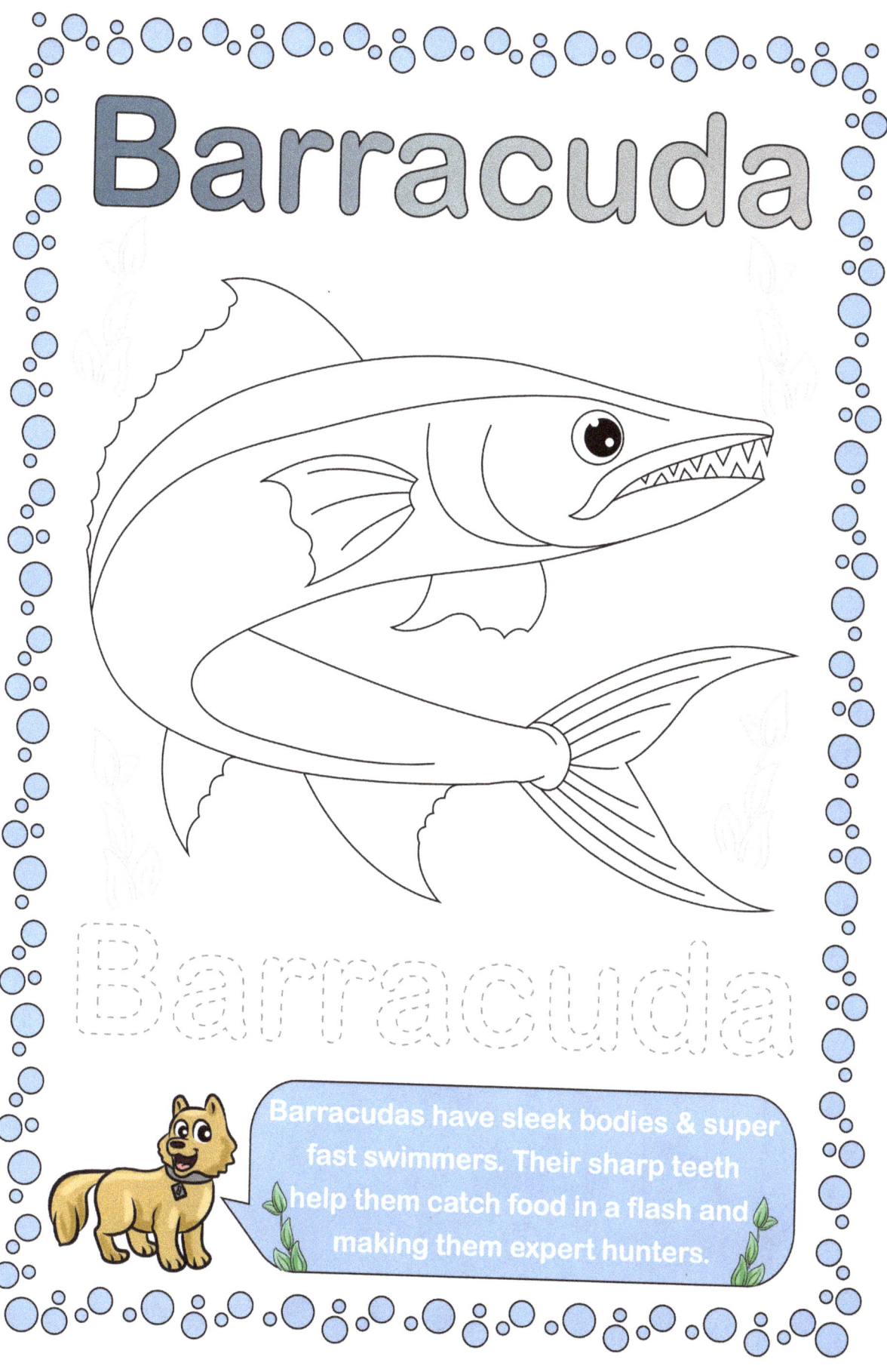

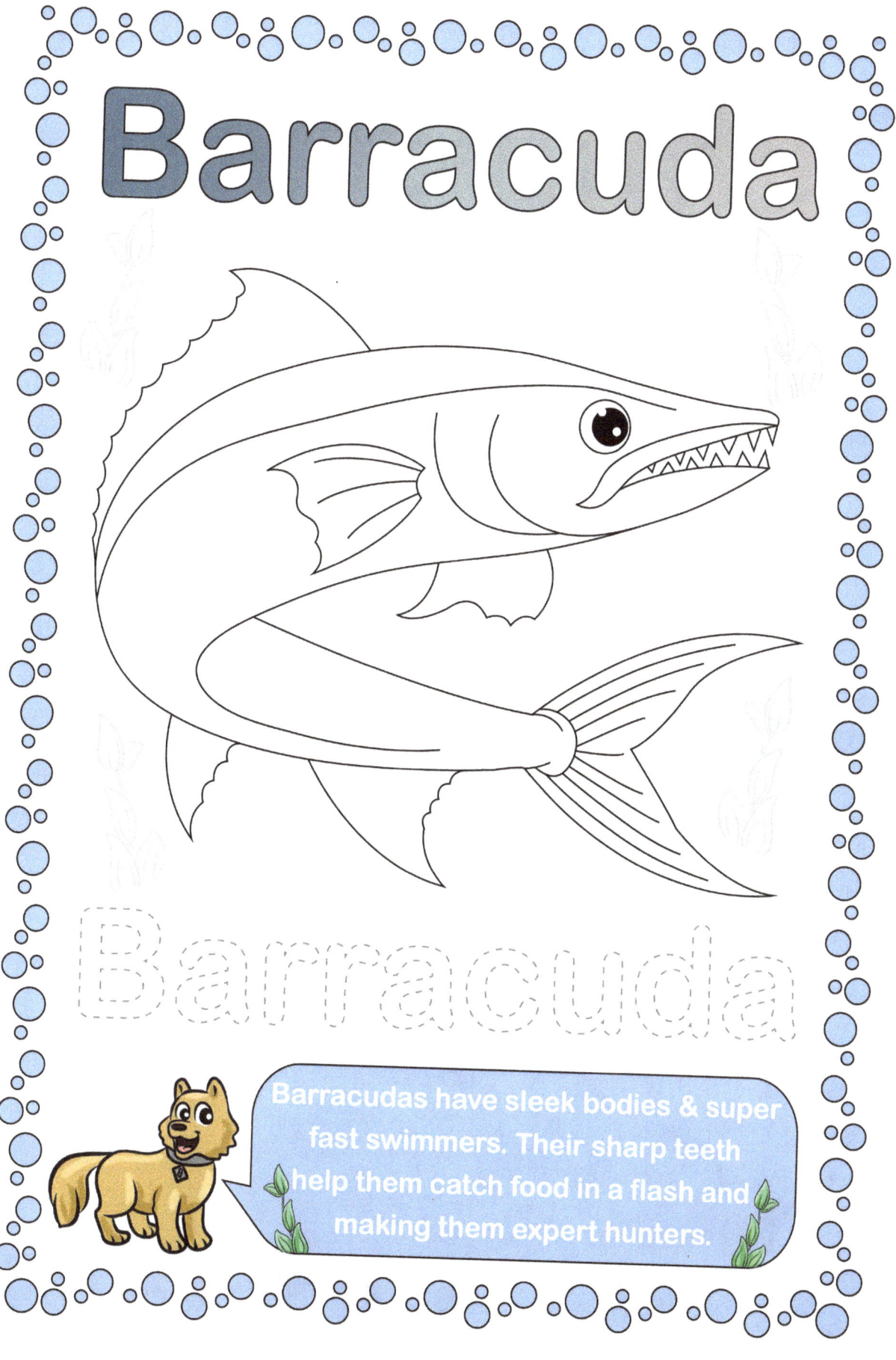

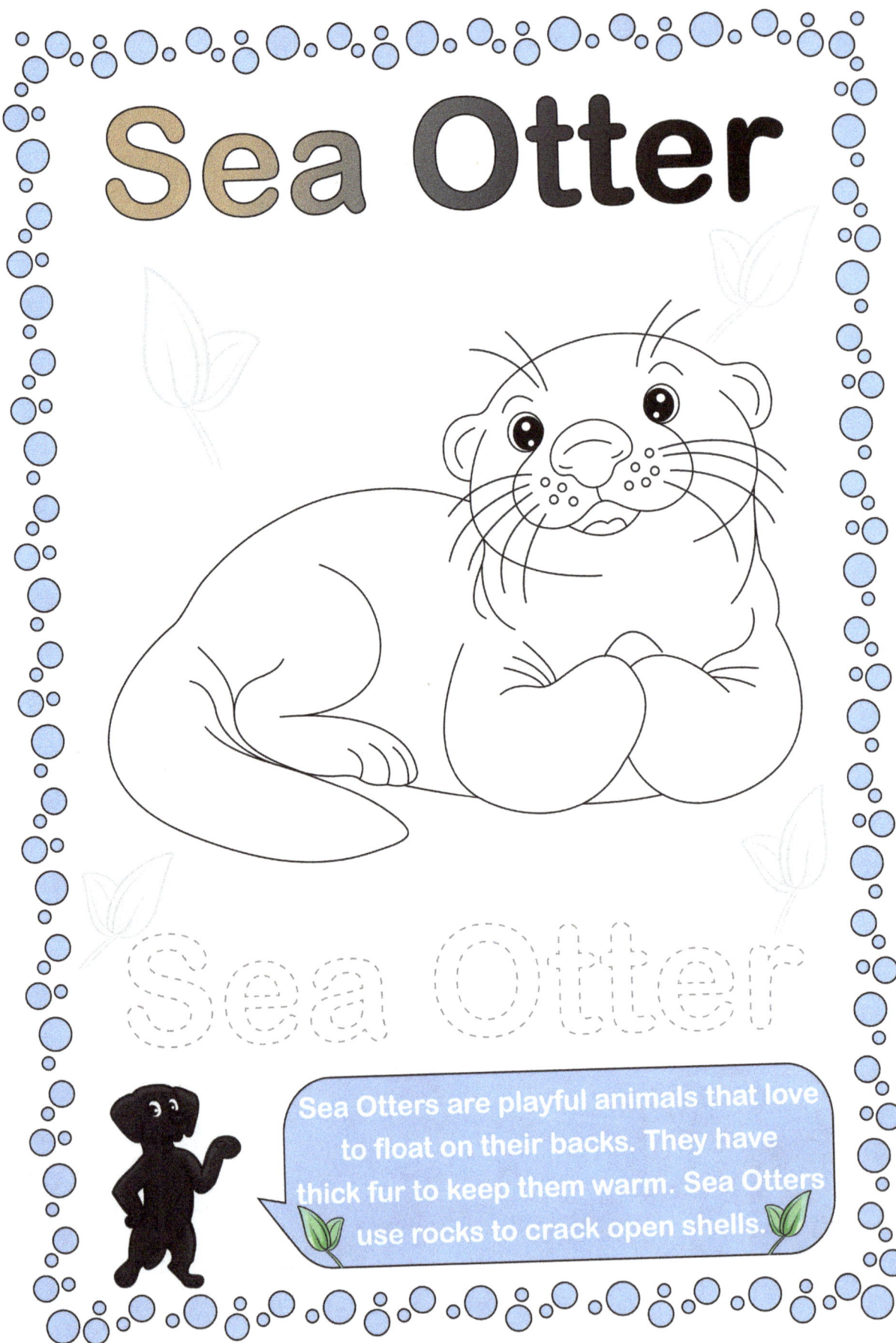